WOD's! The Best Cross Training WOD'S For Beginners

BY TOM CRAIG

A Powerful Step By Step Guide To Integrating Cross Training WOD's Into Your Workout To Lose Weight, Gain Muscle And To Feel Fantastic!

Final Edition

WOD's! The Best Cross Training WOD'S For Beginners Final Edition

Table Of Contents

Introduction

I want to thank you and congratulate you for purchasing the book, *"WODS! The Best Cross Training WOD's for Beginners"*.

This book contains proven steps and strategies on how to integrate Cross Training into your workout routine.

Cross Training shows up in numerous magazines and fitness blogs. Cross Training is unlike any other sport or fitness fad because it does not solely focus on improving a single ability. It aims to develop workouts that target all muscle groups while improving your flexibility, strength, stamina, power, endurance, coordination, balance, agility, speed and accuracy.

While Cross Training athletes are known for their incredible physique. The workouts generally focus on improving overall fitness through varied and challenging workouts. It can be quite intimidating to start Cross Training but it is not as difficult or as dangerous as you might have been lead to believe. It is designed to accommodate different fitness levels and you can gradually increase the weights as you improve.

This book contains all the information that you need to know before staring Cross Training. It gives you an idea about how you can integrate Cross Training into your regular workout regimen. You will also learn the fundamental moves as well as WOD that are suited for beginners. Despite the intense workout that you will have to go through, doing Cross Training is fun and enjoyable. You are presented with exercises that can challenge your body and meet people who share the same passion. While some of the WODs do not require equipment, some do. There is a list of equipment you may need if you are serious in pursuing this regimen. There is also a section for frequently asked questions about this training program.

Thanks again for purchasing this book. I hope you enjoy it!

Chapter 1 Origin Of Cross Training

Technically speaking, Cross Training is the name of a company established in 2000. However, its origin dates back earlier when the company's founder, Greg Glassman, was still a gymnast.

Origin of Cross Training

Glassman observed that athletes who trained with weights and dumbbells became stronger than those who only relied on bodyweight training. Most of his friends would train so hard to be the best in a particular field but would often fall short in other categories. He realized that it is not enough to be an expert in just one field and cross training is essential in improving overall fitness.

Cross Training has the 'jack of all trades, master of none' motto. In Cross Training, the main goal is not to specialize in a particular ability, but to train the body to be strong and fit. Cross Training aims to enhance the 10 physical qualities: cardiovascular endurance, flexibility, power, speed, agility, accuracy, coordination, balance, stamina and strength. A person can develop these qualities by incorporating various movements using different sports and disciplines like weight lifting, gymnastics and running.

Glassman was able to establish a gym in California in 1995; he was also hired to train police officers around the same time, and he also started getting private clients. He was so overbooked that he started training two people at the same time. His clients found it more enjoyable to participate in a group physical activity so the Cross Training community was born. Cross Training was formally recognized in 2000 and has started to branch out after several years.

Origin of the Workouts

Even during its early days, Cross Training has fostered a great community of athletes that come together for competitions. Cross Training can have the same atmosphere of competition.

All of Cross Training workouts bare the name of people to make it easier to remember. There are Girl named WODs and Hero workouts. The latter was dedicated to military, firefighters, army or police that died in the line of the duty. Girl named workouts are benchmarks to gauge the athletes performance and compare it to their previous record.

Over the years, Cross Training has become popular not only because of the Cross Training games but also because it gave a new definition to what 'fitness' means.

A Peek At What You'll Get From Cross Training

- Great community. Unlike regular gyms, you will really get to know people in your Cross Training box. There will always be a feeling of teamwork and support.

- You have constant coaching and support. While you will not have one-on-one coaching, there will always be someone looking out for you.

- Constant improvement. You will be encouraged to beat your personal record and be motivated to improve. You can also advance at your own pace to avoid injuries.

- Gives you a sense of accomplishment. The workouts are always challenging and you might even end up on your back but you will be rewarded with a great sense of accomplishment.

- It is a good outlet. Many athletes do Cross Training to avoid plateaus. It is also a great venue for former athletes who want to compete.

- Mental strength. Pushing through the workouts does not only require physical strength but mental motivation as well.

Basic Cross Training Terms

Box - Cross Training gym

AMRAP - As many repetitions as possible

PR - Personal record

Set - group of repetitions

PB - Personal Best

WOD's! The Best Cross Training WOD'S For Beginners Final Edition

WOD - Workout of the Day

For Time - Do as many repetitions with a limited amount of time

Score - The total amount of repetitions that you completed in a workout

Ass to Grass - It literally means "get as low as you can" or a full depth squat

WODs Cross Training Versus Traditional Gym Workouts

Regardless of your purpose of working out, you might be interested to know how traditional gym workouts and Cross Training differs when it comes to getting rid of fat.
Both can help eliminate the unwanted calories, but they differ in their equipment, structure, and objectives.

The primary objective of working out in the gym is to increase muscle mass and build strength. Carrying out your exercises in the traditional gym can burn more calories than fat, thus by adding more muscles, you will be able to get rid more fat.

Basically, this is done by doing several lifts, known as reps, to complete a set. Lifters may perform one of the 3 sets of a specific workout per weight lifting session.

On the contrary, Cross Training was created to get more generalized objectives of obtaining total fitness. The majority of Cross Training moves includes standard weight lifting exercises, but the goal is not just on improving weight, but likewise on completing more reps in a given length of time.

Most of the weight lifters do their workouts alone or with a personal trainer or with a workout partner in the gyms. There is no uniformity, and weight lifters choose their own exercises and develop their own schemes. Cross Training, on the contrary, prides itself on having a better sense of community.

Even though the exercises are very challenging, Cross Training meets people scalability, and they can modify workouts based on their capability.

The main benefit of weight training is that it develop bone mass among young participants and maintain bone mass in older adults and middle-aged. Weight lifting workouts not only strengthen muscles, but push bones to adapt to the load from the activity, which makes them stronger.

Angelike Norrie a cover model and martial arts expert is a fan of traditional gym workouts, but according to her it only focuses on one to three body parts at a time. But in Cross Training it is the opposite, it promotes an all or nothing scheme.

Cross Training fans would contend that Cross Training can provide these same benefits, although it focuses on strengthening the body in each workout. Cross Training incorporates other activities like running. These activities burn more calories and fat and increased heart rate as compared to weight training.

There are lots of athletes who used Cross Training to prepare them before competing. Cross Training gives them more strength and perspective. It pushes them to the limits and beyond what they can actually do. However, if you don't know your limits and you still attempt to go even further there is a risk of injuries.

The random nature of WOD is not intended for anyone and is not good for injury free lifestyle. You need an expert trainer in performing the reps in time, together with intervals of rowing and sprints.

Chapter 2. Benefits of WODS Cross Training

As mentioned earlier, Cross Training is a combination of vigorous workout regimens with the ultimate goal of enabling you to be totally fit by pushing your body to the max in every aspect. Not only so that you can lift a ton of weight or run a minute mile, but so you are fit to perform anything that life requires you to do. Here are the advantages of engaging in Cross Training.

Intensity

If you are the type of person who stays a lot in the gym, carries out a session of bench presses, intensify it and then proceeds to a light workout, then Cross Training is a serious wake-up call. If the Cross Training workout is a light cup of coffee that wakes you up slowly, this is a shot of 5 hour energy. It is an intense, fast-paced workout that can take less than fifteen minutes a day because that quarter of an hour is going to be reduced, nonstop movement. It may only take 3 to 4 routines, like burpees, squats and a jog, but the idea is that you continue doing each one again through the set time.

It is a concentrated shot of work out and it burns the system – in a good way.

Effort

The key to Cross Training is the power, but hidden in that fact is that you are fundamentally pushing yourself to perform the best you can in each exercise.

Everybody wants result, but not all puts in the effort. In a traditional gym, it is easy cheat reps or take a longer break than required, but because of how the Cross Training workout is created, there is no other choice than to max yourself out.

The key to any workout routine is effort, and since in Cross Training you go balls to the wall, you reach your goals faster.

Short WODs

If you have limited time to work on the treadmill, the Cross Training WODs are what you need. One of the primary advantages of Cross Training is that you can complete in a matter of minutes.

Within a span of 15 or 20 mins, you will be required to complete as many rounds on a particular circuit as you can. By the end of the session, because of the aforementioned effort and intensity, you will have burned more calories as compared to sleepwalking through a regular exercise. It is much faster and is more effective.

Community

Most of the time a gym is simply a collection of random individuals focused on their own different workouts. At a Cross Training box, which is what they know as their gym, it's community.

For beginners, Cross Training is about battling with yourself and not with others. Actually, since the workouts are done in group workouts, the others most of the time encourage you and help you push your limits. Those who complete the workouts last still get a thumbs up for pushing themselves to the limits.

Cross Trainers has one objective in mind: to achieve the best shape possible. And because of that, these people belong in the same group and striving for the same objectives. The camaraderie in Cross Training is part of what makes this workout experience so unique.

Coaching

In a traditional gym, they will simply let you do the workouts on your own. With Cross Training a certified instructors are trained not just to teach and motivate but to help you with your exercises and help modify the workouts around your game. If you have been considering in getting a personal trainer, your Cross Training membership basically includes one.

Multidimensional

The exercises are usually hard to describe since they are so multidimensional. If you are doing Cross Training, you are not only going to the gym to climb up the steps or bulk up. This is not a basic circuit of weightlifting; it is a program that combines various workouts that push all parts of the body to their limits.

Cross Training includes calisthenics, sprints, Olympic weightlifting, gymnastics, plyometrics and several other miscellaneous exercises. If you combine them all, your routine workouts will become more interesting, your body will not get tired of the repetition. Cross Training is constantly changing, which keeps your body and mind from getting bored.

You can Show Your Weak Spot

Since there are lots of challenging aspects of Cross Training, you cannot hide your weaknesses. If you are a power lifter and your main objective of doing this is to get those muscles only then your cardio and conditioning might be exposed. If you are a marathon runner, you will build muscle in different areas.

Boost Metabolism and Increase Muscle Mass

One reason why you should consider a Cross Training workout is that it increase the muscle mass effectively. If you are worrying that you will look like a Hulk at the end, don't be. You don't have the hormones to develop this type of muscle so stop worrying. With Cross Training, you will develop lean muscle that will help accentuate your figure and makes you look toned and defined. Aside from the added muscle mass, it will also boost your metabolic rate that will increase your fat loss progress.

Improved Strength and Functional Fitness

Your strength and functional fitness will improve significantly with Cross Training. It only means that you will not have any trouble completing every activity you need to perform throughout the day. You will see your improvements not only in your body, but in your everyday life as well. For women who choose to maintain a high standard of living as they get older, Cross Training workouts are the best solution.

Improved Cardiovascular Fitness

Cross Training can improve your cardio fitness by carrying out interval training workouts. As compared to other traditional cardio workouts this one is safe and very effective.

Boost Core Strength and Balance

By engaging in a Cross Training workout your core strength and balance will be improved. Most of the workout will throw you slightly off balance and this will get your abs work much harder throughout the workout program. As you continue with the workout scheme, you will keep your balance at all times.

Cross Training Workout is not Boring

Another reason why women should try Cross Training workout is because they are fun. As compared to traditional cardio workout where you need to perform the same repetitive motion again and again, Cross Training can be modified based on your scalability. And because of this you will look forward to every session you are doing, you will not get bored with the routine.

The objective of Cross Training is not to make you super-flexible, super-fast or super-strong, but pretty-fast, pretty-flexible, pretty good and pretty-strong at other things as well. It is the best jack-of-all-trades exercise and nothing gets left behind.

Women Can Do It Too

Some women thought that Cross Training was a guy thing. With the objective of the workout focused on the total physical preparedness against to just bulk strength, women are attracted to it.

If you check out the ratios between male and female, you will be surprised to know that most participants are women, with statistics ranging from 60-40 and even up to 70-30 and women who can complete the Cross Training exercises are going to have amazing bodies.

So, if you are going to the gym to watch cute girls do their workouts, then you might get disappointed. Those cute girls are at the box Cross Trainingting.

Chapter 3. Beginner's Guide

It is quite easy to get intimidated when you see half-naked Cross Trainers lifting weights and jumping on boxes, Cross Training athletes are popular for their great physique and incredible strength. However, these athletes also have to start somewhere. Here are some points to remember before you start Cross Training.

You're competing against yourself

If you're a beginner, don't feel that you need to complete the entire workout on your first day. Make sure to go at your own pace to avoid injury. You'll be building your own strength and flexibility as you train. Chasing after the person next to you can make you lose focus and increase your risk of injury.

Your nutrition is very important

Exercise alone is not enough. Proper nutrition is an essential part of a holistic lifestyle. Eating whole foods can give you the necessary energy to complete your workout. You will only maximize the fitness results if you combine good nutrition and exercise.

You can ask for clarification

Remember that you are investing your time, energy and wellbeing so do not be afraid to ask questions. Make sure that you understand the concept fully and ask questions if you need to. Learning basic Cross Training movements like dead lift, skip or squat takes practice and critique from an expert.

It doesn't get easier, you just get better

The longer you immerse yourself in workouts, the better you will be at it. The human body is capable of adapting to your lifestyle habits. You will notice that you get stronger, flexible or faster, and the workouts will seem easier.

Have fun

Some people see exercise as a tedious chore. You may not even like working out but if you finish it, you would always feel proud and happy. Don't be disappointed if you scored lower than your friends. Remind yourself to have fun and enjoy the competitive atmosphere in the box. You can also start meeting new people with the same hobby. Camaraderie in the gym can foster good and lasting relationships outside.

Do not forget rest and recovery

Many newbies get too excited in training and forget to rest. You should schedule one day in a week to rest. This is when you need to reduce your intensity by half to let your muscles recover.

Learn what a Cross Training class is like

Most Cross Training gyms give free newbie classes. Do not be afraid to try their sessions.

There is usually an introduction class for people who are entirely new at Cross Training. The instructor will usually give a quick overview and show the basic body weight workout.

If you decide to join a workout, the trainer will ask you to go through an on-ramp or elements course. This is to ensure that you know the basic foundational movements of Cross Training. Do not skip this class since it can help you correct your form.

Regular classes are usually 45 minutes to one hour. Everyone starts at the same time and there will be instructors who will be watching to keep track. A regular class has four parts: the warm up, strength work, WOD and cool down.

Cross Training warm-up is different from your regular warm up that usually includes jogging. The dynamic warm up will include jumps, pushups, squats, pull ups and even pull rope. The warm up movements should be able to prepare you for the WOD.

The strength work is where you will do pure strength exercise like dead lifts. If it is not strength day, you will have to work on one skill like muscle ups or pistol squats. WOD is usually the main core of Cross Training classes. Your trainer will tell you to do several exercises in a predefined number of repetitions, or you will have a time limit to do as many repetitions as you can.

The class will end with cool down and stretch. You can stretch on your own or in a group.

Chapter 4. Cross Training Home Gym Equipment

If you are considering setting up a Cross Training gym in your home, you need to invest in the equipment. Creating your own gym does not have to cost a fortune. A popular choice is a garage gym as this will provide you a little more space and will enable for more flexibility with your Cross Training equipment.

Olympic Weightlifting Barbell

Number one on the list of equipment you need to have is an Olympic weightlifting barbell. There is no need for you to purchase the most expensive barbell . If you can purchase a good quality barbell at an affordable price, then good for you.

Cross Training Barbell – you can choose a barbell with or without center knurl. The most common is without center knurl. A pin barbell is a bar with a bolt in the end. For women you can purchase a smaller version of barbell. For kids alumilite barbell, is a good choice. The Bomba Barbell for women has been a favorite for stronger women in the gym.

Bumper Plates

You need a good set of bumpers in your garage gym. You can choose metal plates, but it might damage the concrete floor or rubber matting when you drop it. Rubber bumpers will not damage your floor when you drop them.

Training Bumpers are available in two variations:

Recycled rubber bumpers with HD stainless steel inserts are the Hi Temp bumper plates. These bumpers are made in the USA and is known as the toughest bumper available in the market.

Rubber bumper with Brass Sleeve – there are lots of similar bumpers available in the market – most of them are made in China. The brass inserts will last longer as compared to steel. These are considered as good bumpers but will crack in the long run. Buying cheap ten pound rubber bumpers is not recommended since they will split at the insert after being dropped in your gym.

Pull Up Ring

There are lots of options for this, it is best to start with the pull up bar. Normally, it started out at a local track and utilize the pull up bar. If you want, you can build a pull up rig with pipe from a hardware store for your garage gym or you purchase a 36 inch pre-built version. If you do your exercises outside and prefer a portable version – you can have a simple squat rack or cage where you can hang rings from.

You can get a good set of gym rigs since there is lots thing that you can do with them. Start with pushups, ring dips, muscle-ups and a lot more.

The majority of your Cross Training workouts will have muscle ups and ring dips so you need to be prepared for this. You can make a set of DIY homemade Cross Training rings. It is best to have a set of wood gym rings. Wood rings are smoother when you are doing the multiple reps and may cost the same with plastic rings.

Plastic Gym Rings

The Elite EXF rings receive good reviews and most athletes really love them. The EXF rings have the foam covering on one part of the ring is a little bit irritating as it helps to get a good grip but the foam will wear out over time.

Power Max Fitness Rings

This is a solid setup, however the strapping system is quite complicated, the plastic knurl is very aggressive and the straps are short.

Squat Stands

There are lots of options available here:

Titan squat stands come with a pull up bar on the top similar to a more costly Rogue Fitness rig. It will last longer and is as beefier and less costly. Squat stands take less place and are more mobile.

If you have the skills and time, you can build your own squat stands in wood. If not experts recommend using the Ironmind Squat Stands. However, if you have the budget and place, a Power Rack is a good idea.

York FTS Press/ Squat Stand – very versatile and of great value. It has squat and two j-cups for press. The threads can wear out easily with heavy use so take note of that issue.

ProMaxima – the independent squat stands without connection at the back. This stand is tough and to protect the knurl it has plastic in the cups.

Kettlebell

Experts recommend that you purchase an 8 -16 kg kettlebell for women and a 16-24kg kettlebell for men. This gear is perfect to perform the Cross Training workouts such as Helen. In choosing a kettlebell, keep an eye on the casting seam. Cheap kettlebell has a casting seam that is visible that might hurt your hands.

Medicine Balls and Slam Balls

Medicine balls and slam balls are both weighted balls that you can use to improve your workout routine. The weight of the two balls ranges from 2 lbs to 50 lbs. The size may range from the size of a softball to a little bit larger than a basketball. You can also incorporate these balls to different exercises just by holding the ball while carrying out the exercise. Some workouts include sit-ups, lunges, squats and overhead presses. You can also use the balls for partner exercises such as rotational abdominal work, chest passes and overhead passes.

The slam ball is used for throwing exercises. It has a harder shell made of tough rubber so it can handle a high-velocity impact against a hard surface. For swinging exercises, you can use the slam balls with rope running through the centers. The medicine balls are made of rubber, plastic or leather, and are sometimes designed with handles to make holding the balls easier.

Concept 2 Rowing Machine

Rowing machines are not as popular as the home ellipticals and treadmills, but can be a less expensive choice. You only need around 20 square feet to accommodate a rowing machine in your home gym. The high quality rowing machine is strong enough to support the weight of any use and provide a smooth gliding motion for the seat and an oar to produce the feel of rowing on the water. A low quality row machine may produce a jerky sensation.

Jumping Ropes

There are some new speed ropes like the PowerMax jump rope, and the RxSmart Gear Jump Rope. For beginners with small hands, you can use a ½ inch diameter rope. This type of rope does not require hand strength and is easier to hold onto. Use a shorter length rope – they are easier to maneuver with a full range of motion. For indoor rope, a poly-Dacron rope is a good choice since it does not shed.

Plyo Boxes

A plyo box or plyometric box is a sturdy, wooden or metal platform that is made for lower-body plyometric trainng, which often involves repetitive jumping. To train for a particular sports skills, a small set of plyo boxes like jumping, hurdling, leaping and landing on one leg is used. If you are new to this kind of training, work with a professional trainer before doing it on your own.

For beginners, familiarize yourself with the basics before you can get fancy with different landing and jumping patterns. Start with bilateral exercises which involve landing and jumping on both feet, for instance, box jumps. You can use a higher box once you get familiar with the basics.

GHD Press

The GHD or gluten-ham developer, is a customized bench that supports that hips and holds the ankles down. You can train your hamstrings and lower back by carrying out gluten-ham raises and back hyperextensions. Lying supine in the GHD enables you to do full range of motion sit-ups.

Cross Training Collars

To secure the weights around in the gym, you need a collar. The traditional fashioned spring collars are the best way to start if you are on a budget. If you prefer more you can have muscle clamps to keep your bumpers secured. Either way it is best to have collars in securing the bumper plates on the bar. Most of the Olympic lifters in the traditional school gyms don't use collars, but pick whichever you like.

Most gyms are required to use, lightweight metal collars, which slide over the bar's ends known as sleeves to prevent the plates from slipping off during a lift. In spite adding a few ounces to the barbell's total weight, these collars are tough and should be utilized to stabilize the weighted load. During powerlifting competitions, participants should use the collars that weigh 2.5kgs, which makes the barbell's total weight to 55.115 lbs before the plates are added.

Chapter 5. Basic Moves

Proper form is important in any sport to prevent injuries, and nowhere else is it more important than in Cross Training. Which is why before you start on your first WOD, you need to learn and master the most basic moves.

The Back Squat

The back squat is a great exercise to strengthen your back. The barbell rests across the trapezius muscles. Take a deep breath and pull your stomach in. Push your buttocks back and squat as low as you can. Push back up and think of screwing your feet to the ground.

Pull-ups

Pull-ups are included in many WOD. Start by hanging from a bar. Your hands should be pointing outward in an overhand grip. Make sure to engage your abs as you pull yourself back up until your chin is above the bar.

Pushups

Keep in mind that you can always start on your knees if you find it difficult to use your toes. Begin in a plank position with your feet together. Keep your body in a straight line. Lower your body until the chest touches the floor. Push back up in the starting position. Make sure that your spine stays straight all the time.

Deadlifts

Deadlifts are the foundational movement for strength in many exercise routines. The bar should be on the floor. Pull the bar up but keep it close to your body. Keep your core tight and your hip hinged as you pull the bar to your waist. Squat, lower the bar, and repeat.

Air Squats

Air squat is also referred to as the bodyweight squats. It is a great exercise for all fitness levels. The move can tone your leg, butt, and back muscles. Start by standing with your feet slightly wider than your hips. Turn your toes outward slightly. Pull you shoulder blades together and bend knees to a squat. Lower your thighs until it is parallel to the ground and lift your arms in front of you. Make sure that you also lift your torso. Straighten the legs and lower your arms.

Kettle Bell Swing

Kettle bells are often used in Cross Training. Stand with your feet slightly apart. Place the bell in between your feet. Grip it with your palms facing you. Lower your body and drive through your heel in a quick movement. Swing the kettle bell upward until your arms are stretched in front of you. Make sure to keep you core tight. Shift your weight back to your heels and let the kettle bell swing back to the starting position.

Wall Ball

Wall ball may look like an easy exercise but it is actually difficult. The exercise can help strengthen your muscles and improve your coordination. Start with your feet slightly apart. Lower your butt, but do not push it way back. Throw the ball towards the wall while keeping your elbows close to your body. Aim for a spot on the wall that is slightly higher than your head. Catch the ball with both hands and repeat the movement.

The Burpee

This is a great exercise that can target the major muscle groups in the body. Begin in a starting position with your feet slightly apart. Drop your body in a squat position and both hands on the ground at the same time. Kick your feet back in a plank position. Perform a push up, then quickly jump into a squat position.

Sit ups

Sit ups is a great exercise to strengthen your core. Lie on the floor with your feet flat on the ground. Place hands behind the head. Lift your upper body to your knees but be careful not to strain your neck. Your body should form a V shape. Lower your body to the starting position, then lifts it again.

Lunge

The lunge will help strengthen the legs and core. Make sure to keep your body straight. You shoulders should be relaxed. Pull your bellybutton in to engage your core. Step one leg forward and lower the hips in a 90-degree angle. Your knee should be directly below the ankle. Feel the stretch in your legs as you step forward. Push your feet back to the starting position and repeat on the same leg.

Chapter 6. The Diet of Cross Training

The very foundation of a fit and healthy body is nutrition. There is no shortcut to this. If the body is not receiving essential minerals, vitamins, supplements and nutrients that it needs, other activities and plans geared towards achieving a healthy body are in vain.

Cross Training does not require any special diet. However, in order to succeed in strengthening the body, adding mass to the muscles and providing energy to perform the exercises, here is the list of foods to consume and to avoid by the Cross Training.

What to take in?

1. The Importance of Proteins

The body needs 20 types of amino acids. Eleven of these 20 amino acids are created or produced by the body itself. The remaining 9 needed amino acids, called as essential amino acids, come only through consumption of some foods. These are:

- Tryptophan
- Isoleucine
- Leucine
- Threonine
- Lysine
- Methionine
- Valine
- Phenylalanine
- Histidine

Proteins, when consumed, are broken down into amino acids. Proteins are known as the building blocks of the body. All the internal organs plus the skin, hair, nails, and muscles are built from proteins. A lot of hormones also rely on proteins in order to function effectively. In addition, the digestive and immune systems also need adequate amount of proteins to work correctly. Not to mention, for blood to be healthier, it needs proteins, too.

Growing kids and teenagers would definitely benefit from additional protein consumption, as they would need every bit of it during their crucial growing up years. In the same manner, pregnant women are oftentimes advised to increase intake of proteins to support the growth and development of the fetus.

Cross Trainers know that proteins are important, which is why they give extra attention to them. The development and proper functioning of many body parts are reliant on protein intake. Plus, the building, repairing and maintaining of lean body mass require adequate protein consumption. All these things are essential for Cross Trainers.

However, the body is not that good in storing proteins compared in storing fats and glucose. Hence, replacement of proteins through consumption of protein-rich foods is essential. If there were inadequate proteins, the body would compensate the lack by breaking down muscles to acquire the needed proteins.

For Cross Trainers, their caloric requirement would be 30% proteins, coming from lean and varied proteins. Here are the recommended high-quality dietary protein sources.

> Lean beef and veal

> Beans

> Nonfat or Low-fat Greek yogurt

> Cottage cheese

> Eggs

> Bacon

> Fish (Salmon, Tuna, Halibut)

> Tofu

> Lentils

> Lean chicken and turkey

> Milk and soymilk

> Nuts (such as pistachios, peanuts, almonds)

> Seeds (pumpkins, squash, flaxseed, watermelon seeds and sunflower seeds)

It goes without saying that hardcore athletes, or those that do heavy workouts would require more proteins. The use of powder protein supplements is not rare among these athletes to provide their protein requirement. When checking the label, make sure that the protein powder supplement is high in leucine as this is vital in making the muscles strong, powerful and bigger.

2. Carbohydrate Requirements of Cross Trainers

Among the food groups, carbohydrate is the most controversial. There have been many write-ups of how evil it is, and how it only does bad things to the body. However, there are also many positive feedbacks on its benefits. Which is which?

There are predominantly two types of carbohydrates and this is where the confusion usually arises. The two types are the simple and the complex carbohydrates. The chemical structure of the simple carbohydrates causes them to be digested easily and absorbed by the body very quickly. This can lead to hyperglycemia or increased blood glucose, which in turn, can spike the blood insulin levels. This is not good for the body and is often the culprit for the development of the dreaded Diabetes disease.

Examples of foods that are classified as simple carbohydrates are:

> Candies

> Sodas

> Table sugar

> Fruit juice

> Cakes

> Anything made with white flour (bread, pastas, baked goods)

> ➤ Packaged cereals
>
> ➤ Some fruits and vegetables

On the other hand, complex carbohydrates take more time to digest and absorb, thus the risks for diabetes and other heart diseases are lower. In addition, most complex carbohydrates are high in fiber and other nutrients, vitamins and minerals, which the body needs.

Examples of healthy complex carbohydrates are:

> ➤ Spinach
>
> ➤ Whole barley
>
> ➤ Turnip greens
>
> ➤ Lettuce
>
> ➤ Apples
>
> ➤ Grapefruit
>
> ➤ Asparagus
>
> ➤ Oatmeal
>
> ➤ Dried apricots
>
> ➤ Okra
>
> ➤ Celery
>
> ➤ Yams
>
> ➤ Carrots
>
> ➤ Potatoes
>
> ➤ Soybeans
>
> ➤ Radishes
>
> ➤ Soybeans
>
> ➤ Buckwheat
>
> ➤ Zucchini

Generally speaking, Cross Trainers should try to limit or avoid simple carbohydrates and make complex carbohydrate as their main source of carbohydrate. However, there is another thing that one must take into consideration about carbohydrates, and that is the glycemic index.

Not all simple carbohydrates are bad for the body and not all complex carbohydrates are good for the body. Some simple carbohydrates are low-glycemic while some complex carbohydrates are high-glycemic. What is this glycemic index? Originally, this index was created to monitor what carbohydrate is best for the diabetics. Later on though, many athletes, body builders and health buffs resort to glycemic index to determine their carbohydrate requirements.

Glycemic index identifies which carbohydrate breaks down easily and causes the quick release of glucose in the blood. High glycemic index (high GI) carbohydrates can cause sugar in the bloodstream to spike, causing insulin levels to rise, too, while low GI does the opposite. However, glycemic index is affected by various factors such as other foods taken aside from carbohydrates, amount of food and activities of the person thus it would be difficult to isolate and specify high GI foods to low GI foods. In general though, low glycemic carbohydrates are better than high glycemic carbohydrates.

The caloric requirement for carbohydrates of a Cross Trainingter is at 40%.

3. Fats in the Diet of the Cross Trainers

Fats comprise the last 30% caloric requirement of a Cross Trainingter. Like the carbohydrates, this has garnered many controversies, too. Many doctors and nutritionists have advocated the low-fat diet. They believe this to be the key to lowering risks to cardiovascular diseases, losing weight and managing blood pressure and cholesterol. However, the amount of fats is not the main culprit but the type of fats.

Fats can be healthy and unhealthy. Bad fats make one prone to many diseases. They are known to adhere to the blood vessels and accumulate, causing blockage to the passageway of blood. This can lead to hypertension, CAD (coronary artery disease) and various heart ailments.

Here is the list of unhealthy fats, which a Cross Trainingter needs to avoid or eliminate from his diet.

Saturated fats or Saturates – these include prepared or packaged foods labeled with hydrogenated oils, fatty meals, butter, lard, full-fat dairy products, cocoa butter, coconut oil and palm oil, to name a few.

Trans fats – include foods that are made with partially hydrogenated vegetable oil, most snack foods and ready-prepared foods.

On the other hand, healthy oils or fats protect one's heart and enhance total wellbeing. They are comprised of the following:

Monounsaturated fats or monounsaturates – olive, peanut and canola oils are included in the list plus avocados, nuts, seeds and non-hydrogenated margarines.

Polyunsaturated fats or polyunsaturates – under this category are omega-6 fats and omega-3 fats. Included for omega-6 fats are safflower, sunflower, corn and sesame oils, nuts and seeds. For omega-3 fats, fattier fish, soybean and canola oils, omega-3 eggs, walnuts and flaxseeds.

Foods to Avoid

Eating right means avoiding processed foods and sweets as much as possible. Although Cross Training does not totally require its followers to give up certain foods, it is advantageous for the body to limit to the barest minimum the consumption of these two food items.

Dangers of processed foods

They are aptly called "slow killers" as they quietly and gradually do the following things to the body:

> ➢ Disrupt blood sugar level. Processed foods have high sugar and refined carbohydrate contents. Blood sugar spikes up upon consumption of these foods, which in turn will stimulate the release of insulin from the pancreas. Continuous increase and decrease of both insulin and glucose levels can damage the endocrine system. Development of Diabetes Mellitus has higher probability because of this disruption.

> Add unwanted pounds in the weighing scale. Processed foods can make one overweight or worse, obese. Satiety or feeling of fullness is not readily felt when one consumes these foods. The tendency is to eat more. This is because most of these foods just have empty calories. They fill the stomach but they do not supply the needed nutrients, minerals and vitamins of the body. They have low nutritional value. In addition, they also leave the person with false feel-good effect each time he eats, causing him to want to eat more.
> Susceptibility to diseases such as cancer, kidney problems and allergic reactions due to its artificial ingredients. Processed foods usually have high contents of preservatives or additives such as Butylated hydroxyanisole (BHA). This ingredient has been linked to the development of these diseases.
> Increased risk of problems in the excretory system. Processed foods are typically low in fiber. This makes it harder for the body to remove waste products. The longer these waste products stay inside the body, the more damage they could do to the body. Hence, daily defecation is recommended.
> More prone to cardiovascular diseases, specifically hypertension and atherosclerosis (formation of blockages along the arterial wall) due to its high trans fats content.

Have you ever wondered why some processed foods are difficult to give up, even though you are aware of their dangers? Addictive property is found among processed foods. One gets hooked to chips, sodas, rice, and canned goods, to name just a few, because of this. Sometimes, withdrawal symptoms are experienced when the person tries to remove these items from the diet. There would be headaches, tremors, nausea and vomiting, depression, loss of appetite, fatigue and shakiness.

Sweet deception

Simple sugar is also known as sweet poison. It does exactly what real poison does to the body, albeit in an extremely enjoyable way. Just like processed foods, it would take several years for the bad effects of sugar to manifest in the body. When it does, it is usually too late for the person to do anything. He is already afflicted with various diseases because of excessive intake of simple sugars.

Unknown to many people, simple sugar can do the following things to your body:

> Damage the heart. Sugar has a molecule known as glucose metabolite glucose 6-phosphate or G6P that could alter the muscle protein of the heart. This affects the pumping ability of the heart, which later on could lead to heart failure and death. For a Cross Trainingter, having a healthy heart is vital in the accomplishment of the exercises. It is therefore wise to eliminate simple sugars in the diet when one is serious with Cross Training and health, in general.

> Disrupt Leptin – the hunger hormone. This hormone's primary function is regulation of hunger and satiety. However, excessive and frequent intake of simple sugars can make the leptin gauge faulty. Therefore, even when a person is already full, the hormone would fail to signal the body to stop eating, leading to increased weight.

Another function of leptin is related to energy expenditure of the body. Upon reaching a certain threshold, leptin will encourage the body to engage in some physical activities. However, when leptin is low, it will cause the body to feel tired and resort to resting instead. The tendency of the person to exercise or not is also dependent on leptin. Hence, Cross Trainers would find excessive consumption of simple sugars to be a big disadvantage on their goal of performing WODs.

> Makes one susceptible to development of cancer. Glucose and insulin always go hand in hand. The formation of the hormone known as GIP is triggered by sugar intake. A protein called B-catenin controls this GIP hormone. This protein, in turn, is linked to insulin becoming resistant. Recent studies have shown the connection between insulin resistance and formation of cancer.

As with processed foods, Cross Trainers should avoid these sweet temptations at all times. Not only will doing this protect them from various diseases but it will also improve their performances in accomplishing WODs.

Other Tips

Meal planning is important among Cross Trainers. This is an indication that the Cross Trainingter is serious in his aspiration of becoming healthy and strong. When one takes time to sit down and prepare his menu for a week, a month or a quarter, this reflects his determination to be successful in this endeavor. The upside of doing meal planning is that it also saves him time and money.

Prior to dietary modification, here are some recommended actions for the Cross Trainers to take:

1. As a standard safety precaution, one should inform his primary health care provider of his plan to change his diet. This is to ensure that no medical condition or pharmacological management will be affected with the diet.
2. Inform family members, friends and significant others of the decision to modify the diet. They can help the individual avoid the unhealthy foods and at the same time, they can act as his cheerleaders, especially during trying times.
3. Temptations to succumb to the previous diet will be eliminated when the unhealthy foods are not available. Hence, cleaning one's ref, cupboard, and other food storage can help the individual overcome his tendency to rivet back to his old diet. Remove all the simple and high glycemic carbohydrates that are in there. Remove all processed foods, too. As much as possible, choose fresh, raw, organic foods only.

Here are other tips to avoid the hunger pangs and cravings for simple carbohydrates during the first few days or weeks of the dietary modification.

1. Have a filling breakfast. This will supply the needed energy of the body for the whole day.
2. Have a light dinner. Instead of meats or chicken dishes, prepare stir vegetables, salads or soups. Dinners are preferably taken three hours prior to sleeping.
3. Always have healthy snacks stashed in the bag. It is expected that one will feel hungry in between meals, especially in the first few days. Having fruits, nuts or snack bars would eliminate the temptation to buy prepared foods or fast foods.

4. Increase fluid intake. This is not only effective in making one feel full but it also helps eliminate toxins in the body. If increased intake of fluids is not contraindicated to the person, the minimum water intake is at 10 glasses per day.
5. Be experimental and inventive. Look for new recipes. Try new healthy ingredients.
6. Do not totally deprive one's cravings. It can have a negative effect on one's emotions. One can enjoy desserts (even chocolates, preferably dark chocolates) every other day. Depriving oneself can backfire, which can lead to consumption of generous amounts of sweets and simple carbohydrates.
7. Have high-protein meals during activities and exercises. Consume adequate amount of carbohydrates too to supply extra energy to the body during workouts.

Intermittent Fasting (IF) for Cross Trainers

This may come as a surprise but intermittent fasting is also recommended once in a while among Cross Trainers. This is the time that the body will detoxify all the toxins accumulated. This simply means that the Cross Trainingter will sometimes miss meals, whether for 12, 16 or 24 hours, and then eat again after the allotted time of fasting. The best time to do fasting is when has no work or classes, which is probably during the weekends.

Intermittent fasting has been found very beneficial for the Cross Trainers. Aside from giving the digestive system enough time to rest, rejuvenate, repair and reproduce cells and tissues, it also provides the following advantages:

➢ Reduction of:

o Blood lipids, such as LDL (low density lipoproteins or the bad cholesterol) and triglycerides.

o Blood pressure, which is probably due to the changes in the sympathetic and parasympathetic activities.

o Markers of inflammation, which include C-reactive protein (CRP), tumor necrosis factor (TNF) and brain-derived neurotropic factor (BDNF).

o Risks of cancer.

- o Oxidative stress.
- ➤ Increase of:
  - o Cellular turnover
  - o Metabolic rate
  - o Burning of fats
- ➤ Enhancement of:
  - o Appetite
  - o Cardiovascular function
  - o Glucose-insulin blood levels
  - o Immune system

Tips in doing IF

1. Reminder again – inform the doctor of this intention. It may interfere with pharmacological or non-pharmacological management of existing disease or condition.
2. Start slowly. Try missing one meal first (preferably dinner) once a month. Then gradually increase the time and frequency of fasting as tolerated.
3. Drink plenty of fluids while fasting.
4. Schedule the fast on rest days from exercise or heavy workouts.

Final thoughts on nutrition for Cross Trainers

Diet and exercise go hand and hand. When properly executed, this two could result to ideal body weight, stronger bones and muscles, a healthier body and longer life span. Not to mention, they both could help improve the emotional aspect of the individual, making him more confident and less prone to depression. Studies have shown that proper diet and exercise can curb the negative effects of stress. How? Through the release of the "feel good" chemicals in the brain as stimulated by the activities done and the healthy foods consumed.

Cross Training is a lifestyle and so does proper nutrition. They may seem overwhelming at first but the benefits are worth it. As the body gets used to these changes, it will become natural and effortless to do these exercises and to consume these healthy foods in no time at all.

Chapter 7 Lifestyle of the Cross Trainers

Being healthy, having a strong body and having the ability to perform various activities such as the ones being presented in Cross Training do not happen magically while one lives unhealthy lifestyle. Something has to give and in this case, it's the wrong living practices. Some of the Cross Trainers may think that this is too much to ask for. After all, when one is used to a certain kind of living, modifying or altering it may take some effort and difficulty.

There is no going around this, however. Unhealthy vices defeat the purpose of Cross Training plus it would almost seem impossible for a Cross Trainingter to successfully accomplish the WODs if they are practicing vices such as the following:

Smoking

Various studies have confirmed the hazardous effects of smoking in the body. In fact, it has been named as the number one cause of preventable deaths in America, with an estimated 480,000 deaths per year. This is not surprising as there are hundreds of harmful ingredients in a single stick of cigarette, with the addicting nicotine of top of the list. Aside from this, there are around 4000 chemicals that are found in cigarette smoke, with 43 of them carcinogenic or cancer-causing.

Smoking negatively affects nearly all the organs of the body. It makes the person more susceptible to various diseases, including cancers. It decreases the years and the quality of life.

A Cross Trainingter who smokes would have difficulty achieving WODs because of the following:

> ➢ Respiratory problems – there is difficulty in breathing or shortness of breath during workouts. Also, since nicotine causes vasoconstriction or narrowing of the blood vessels, there is inadequate supply of oxygenated blood to various organs, making it harder for the body to function normally as one does WODs.

> ➢ Cardiovascular problems – smoking has increased the risk of developing cardiovascular diseases up to 2-4 times. People

suffering from heart ailments may not be able to tolerate some of the activities of Cross Training.

➢ Skeletal system – smoking has adverse effects on the bones, cartilages and joints of the person, too. This can hinder his ability to perform WODS.

➢ Muscular weakness – as the muscle are deprived of oxygen because of the effects of smoking, muscle growth and strength are hindered.

➢ Overall performance and endurance – smoking diminishes energy levels, leaving one feeling fatigued and weak. Therefore, there is less time for exercise. The intensity of one's exercise is also affected.

Smoking cessation and Cross Training

Although Cross Training is not designed as a smoking cessation program, it has helped thousands of smokers to quit this vice. How?

1. Cross Training has broken the routine. For example, someone who used to smoke as soon as he wakes up now has to attend to his WODS, first thing in the morning. As he gets used to not smoking in the morning, the addiction will gradually diminish too. Soon, he will not crave for cigarettes even in the afternoon until he totally overcomes it.

2. The Cross Trainingter is motivated to be healthy and to stay that way. As the benefits of being healthy are experienced, the Cross Trainingter would want to maintain that feeling permanently.

3. The strong support system. The community of Cross Trainers can help the person overcome his vice through constant reminder, encouragement and support.

Drinking alcoholic beverages

Alcohol is absorbed in the bloodstream quite immediately after consumption. From the bloodstream, it will go to the liver to be metabolized or broken down. Unfortunately, it takes hours before an ounce of alcohol is metabolized in the liver hence it stays and saturates the blood instead.

Alcohol is known to be a diuretic, meaning it removes fluids from your body. Therefore, dehydration can take place. Less fluids plus more alcohol in the blood is not compatible with how the body is designed. This could negatively affect the functions of the cells, tissues and organs. At the same time, alcohol can affect the release and production of hormones, which in turn, can cause havoc to the whole system of the person.

Another bad outcome of drinking alcohol is making one malnourished. Alcohol has zero nutrients. This is called as empty calories. Therefore, the body feels full but it has not received any nutrient at all. Ironically, the alcoholic becomes fat. How? These empty calories are the first ones being burned by the body and used for energy. Other calories, especially from carbohydrates, are unused and are therefore stored as fats in the body.

Another disadvantage is that it can cause havoc on one's sleeping pattern too. A more detailed discussion on the importance of sleep and rest will be touched later on in this chapter.

Cross Training and Alcohol

These two things do not go well together, too. Aside from the enumerated harms that alcohol can bring to a person, a Cross Trainingter would do well to avoid alcohol because of the following reasons:

1. Alcohol affects protein synthesis. What is protein synthesis? It is a process where biological cells (primarily amino acids) generate or form new proteins. As muscles are made or built from proteins, any disruption or delay in this process can hinder the growth of the muscles. Alcohol can cause 20% reduction in the speed of the process of protein synthesis.

2. It lowers production and release of testosterone. This hormone is the one responsible for building muscles hence any problem in this hormone would affect the muscular system as a whole.

3. It causes dehydration. Muscles are comprised of 70% water. It goes without saying how damaging lack or inadequate fluids is to the body.

4. Alcohol causes elimination of minerals, vitamins and electrolytes. Many of these substances are expelled from the body through urination.

Note: Once in a while, there would be occasions where one has no choice but to have a glass or two of an alcoholic drink. Minimal amounts of alcohol taken infrequently would not affect one's Cross Training training that much. It's all right to enjoy a drink when there is a need to.

Not having adequate time for sleep and rest

Rest and sleep are considered as luxuries to this fast-paced generation. Most people are always on the go, with slogan such as "sleeping is for the weak" becoming popular. Is there a connection between athletic performance and good sleep? Researches have shown that sleep is not only vital for improved athletic performance but also for general health maintenance. The recommended number of hours of sleep is 9 per night.

The benefits of having enough rest and sleep are:

1. Healthy brain function. Sleep improves learning. It also enhances memory retention and decision-making skills. In addition, a good night sleep helps one to be more focused on the tasks and be creative in solving problems.

2. Emotional wellbeing. Sleep deficient people are crankier. They tend to relate poorly with others. Hence, having enough sleep is great for one's social life. Studies revealed that lack of sleep has been linked to depression and suicide.

3. Physical health. Sleep is the time when the body recuperates. Therefore, when there is a deficit in sleep, healing and repair of vital organs such as the heart, kidneys, liver, among other things are missed. The risk to develop and acquire diseases of heart, kidney and brain are increased. There is also higher susceptibility for diabetes and stroke.

4. Growth and development. The body is stimulated to release the growth hormones when there is enough rest and sleep.

5. Daytime performance. One's ability to function well in daytime is also dependent on the amount of hours spent sleeping during

the night. Simple tasks such as driving, studying, memorizing are affected depending whether one has enough or lack of sleep. Poor performance, poor ability to decide, slower reaction time and proneness to commit mistakes have all been linked to deficiency of sleep.

Cross Training and Sleeping

Sleeping for Cross Trainers is a must. On top of the mentioned benefits, Cross Trainers need 8-9 hours of deep sleep. Here are five reasons for this:

1. Carbohydrate cravings are stimulated with lack of sleep. Glucose and insulin levels are disrupted when one succumbs to the cravings for simple carbohydrates. In turn, the energy levels, moods and performance of the Cross Trainingter are negatively affected as well.

2. Lack of sleep can also lead to increased blood pressure. When there is presence of hypertension, rest instead of exercise, is recommended.

3. There is lack of drive and energy. Instead of waking up enthusiastic and alert, the person feels tired already and does not feel like exercising or doing anything productive.

4. Presence of mood swings. Sleep deprived individuals are prone to easy irritability and changes in moods. This could affect the ambiance and mood of the whole team.

When it comes to rest and sleep, it is not just about the length (or number of hours) of sleep only but also about the quality of sleep. To ensure a good night sleep, here are some tips that one can follow:

➢ Set a regular time for sleeping. The body is used to routines. When it gets the pattern for sleeping, it tends to feel sleepy at the designated time. When there is no set time for sleeping, the body would not be able to signal itself to take the time to rest and sleep.

➢ Avoid stimulants such as coffee, cigarette, chocolates, sweets and alcohol prior to sleeping. Also, meals should be taken at least three hours prior to sleeping.

> Sleep in a dark and quiet room. This makes one's sleep deeper and longer. Remove distractions such as television, cellphones or books.

> Have a relaxed mind. Do not bring paper works, problems and other issues in the bedroom. Make it a place solely for resting.

A person may not have enough time for many things but he should make time for resting and sleeping. This is especially true for serious Cross Trainers.

Not managing stress

According to statistics, 85-90% of medical conditions are stress-related. Stressors (the agents causing the stress) are neutral. The person's response to stress is the decisive factor of who will be healthier, physically, emotionally, socially and even intellectually.

Take for instance being stuck in a heavy traffic. That could be a real stressor for some while it could be relaxing for others. How one views the stressor will determine his response to it. If he perceives it as a stressor, cortisol (stress hormones) are released that could cause the following to the body:

> Increased heart rate, respiratory rate and temperature

> Shoot up of blood pressure

> Disturbed sleep pattern

> Depression

> Inability to focus, decide or think properly

> Increased blood sugar

> Upset digestive system

> Depressed immune system

> Infertility

Aside from these, even relationships with workmates or family members can be strained when faced with stress. The best thing to do is to learn how to manage one's stress.

Nowadays, there are many options that one could utilize to keep stress from greatly affecting the person. Here are some of them:

1. Identify the stress triggers. When the person knows what his stressors are, he would be able to avoid them or plan on how to tackle them.

2. Try these simple stress-reduction strategies such as deep breathing, yoga, massage or meditation. Studies have proven that taking deep breaths while in a stressful situation can make the person calm by as much as 30%. This effect is attributed to adequate distribution of oxygenated blood to vital organs, primarily to the brain, when one is doing breathing exercises. Yoga, on the other hand, helps fight stress as it brings physical and mental disciplines to the inner self to achieve peace and serenity.

3. Visualization. This is the positive use of imagination. Instead of dwelling on the negative circumstances that are causing the stress, think of beautiful and relaxing thoughts. This way, the focus would be shifted from the situation to the relaxing thoughts.

4. Smile. Even though there are no reasons to smile or laugh, do so. This releases endorphins, the "feel good" chemicals in the body, helping relieve the stress. Smiling also strengthens the immune system, making the person less prone to various sicknesses.

5. Compose a mantra. Saying short, positive and comforting words or phrases can easily relieve one of stress. Examples are "all is well", "I can handle this", "I feel calm" or whatever it is that you want to say.

6. Have sex with your espouse. Sex has been discovered to be a great stress buster. It releases endorphins, serotonin and other feel good chemicals. Plus, it helps lower blood pressure, too. Sex has been discovered to strengthen the immune system, also. Having frequent sex will not only improve one's marriage relationship but it will also enhance one's health.

7. Take a walk. Doing this will relieve one of stress because:

a. It puts the brain in a meditative state. The best place to take a walk is in a park or where there are lots of trees and green plants. Why? An "involuntary attention" is triggered when one walks through green spaces, making the mind more receptive to its surrounding rather than to the stresses at hand.

b. It provides more energy to the person. As much as 20% energy is supplied when one starts to take a walk. This excess energy can later be used to solve problems or manage stress.

c. It improves circulation, allowing perfusion of oxygenated blood to the brain and other vital organs.

d. It releases endorphins, therefore one feels good and stress is relieved.

8. Play with your pets. Studies have shown that pets are great antidotes for stress. As much as 37% stress reduction takes place when one plays with his pet. This could be attributed to the shift of attention from the current worries to the pet's playfulness. Researches have discovered that spending even 5 minutes with one's pet can decrease the release of stress hormone, increase the release of oxytocin hormone (the hormone linked to relaxation and happiness), lower blood pressure and lessen stress and anxiety.

9. Verbalize your stress to your loved ones. Another powerful tool to fight stress is just having a talk with a loved one. Being able to express all the worries and concerns in the inside of the person with someone who is willing to listen is a great stress reducer. Others have found this strategy very effective in finding the solution for the problem, too. Oftentimes, it is when they are describing the problem that solutions come to them.

10. Practice mindfulness. Transferring the focus from the problem to another object is also another way of relieving stress. How to do this? Simply concentrate and focus on a particular object. It could be a body part, one's breathing or other external objects. It could also be a mental picture or a mantra. When the attention is shifted away from stress,

calmness comes and later on, the person will be able to attend to the stress with a relaxed and calm mind.

11. Call a friend. Stress need not to be faced alone. The stronger the support system one has, the higher the probability of him overcoming the stress. When one feels overwhelmed with a situation, it is best to ask for assistance from a friend or a loved one. Sometimes, a simple phone call is all that it takes to become relax and calm.

12. Calm your spirit by doing something spiritual like saying a prayer, meditating, or reading spiritual books or articles. Studies show that those who are spiritual tend to be calmer and healthier, and are better at managing their stress.

Cross Training as Stress Reducer

Cross Training can actually help relieve a person from stress. As discussed earlier, exercising causes the endorphins, serotonin and oxytocin to be released. These hormones make the person feel good about himself, with others, with his surroundings and life in general. Plus, these hormones work as analgesic too. They can relieve pain. When one is free from bodily and even mental pains, sleep comes easily. This in turn, will help reduce stress and stabilize the person.

Cross Training is found to reduce fatigue also. This gives the person added energy to face the situation and solve the problem. It makes him attentive, alert and enthusiastic. It also enhances cognitive function, allowing the mind to be more creative in finding the solutions to the problems at hand.

Cross Training helps elevate and stabilize moods, improve concentration and alertness and help decrease overall tension and stress. It is a great anti-anxiety therapy.

To sum it up, Cross Training is equivalent to a healthy lifestyle. It is not a mere fad where after several months, one goes back to his previous unhealthy life practices. There must be a permanent change. Along with this change come the permanent benefits, too.

Chapter 8. WOD for Beginners

This high-intensity workout program can work not only for men, but for women as well, not only for the young ones, but even to your grandparents. All WODs or Cross Training workouts are scalable to each person's fitness capability. From bodyweight-only workouts to exercises with weights, your WOD as a beginner does not have to be scary. But it should be able to challenge and change you.

Although the true Cross Training experience will normally take place at the local box along with a team of athletes on your side, it is still possible to do the workouts anywhere on your own. These beginner friendly but challenging Cross Training workouts will inspire you to join the program.

Cross Training Half Cindy

10 min, AMRAP
5 pull ups
10 push-ups
15 air squats

Athletes perform Full Cindy for twenty minutes, and since you are just a beginner, you will start at 10 minutes. You might experience some difficulties rising from the ground to do another round of push-ups after one round. Because your body is not familiar with the strength required for many WODs. By performing half the time, you are diminishing returns. You will discover what your body is capable to do and how fast you hit tiredness. And with that comes the significance of form.

Your form deteriorates as you start to get tired, in which case, you can make some changes. To change this WOD, an elastic band is used in covering the bar that can be used for assisted pull-ups. You can do push-ups on your knees. Count your reps and take note, so you can check your progress.

Cross Training Total

5 back quats

3 overhead presses
3 deadlifts

Don't get intimidated by these heavy lifts, they will make you stronger. This WOD focuses on enabling a beginner to get familiar with the heavy lifting element of the sport. The work is not timed; it is about determining how the weight affects your body and how much weight you move safely. Five squats will help you get used to feeling the weight on your shoulders in case you haven't done it in the past.

Form is vital for this workout of the day. If you are not sure how to perform the lift, ask an expert or a trainer for help. The expert also recommends to take a video of yourself while performing the exercise and send it to fellow Cross Trainingter for suggestions and pointers. The primary priority of Cross Training is staying safe.

Note: since you are new to these lifts, this workout of the day is about familiarizing yourself with the feel and form. As soon as you become comfortable with it, you will do the Cross Training Total as if it is done in the games – 3 attempts to lift the heaviest load successfully on each movement. Your third attempt which is the heaviest lifts, get combined to produce your Total. And as there is still no time limit, you need to complete all 3 attempts for one lift before getting into the next.

Helen WOD

3 rounds, For Time
400 m run
21 kettle bell swings
12 pull ups

Running seems to be an easy workout, but don't take this one lightly. On the first one don't go as fast as you can because you will wear out yourself. You'll give up after one round. The most important thing here is to build endurance and it usually takes time to build. Cross Training will teach you how to handle your body. You can modify this WOD; try Russian Kettlebell swings if you are not able to safely swing the weight overhead. Use a resistance band to cover the bar to add resistance, for pull-ups, or if in case your strength is not there yet, you can perform ring rows.

Wall Ball and Burpees

21-15-9, For Time
Wall balls
Burpees

You might be wondering why 21, 15, 9 rep? There is no definite reason; however, by the time you get to nine reps,it is guaranteed to feel as hard as 21 did. Also, the 21, 15, 9 scheme can be broken down into rounds of 3 this mean – 21 is 3 rounds of seven reps, 15 would be three rounds of five and nine would be three of three. This will break up the reps and gives you a breather – which is allowed and recommended.

The combination wall ball-burpees is a good one in the worst way possible. If you perform it once, it's like the wall ball is all leg, and the burpees are all arms, however, these workout works on the shoulder muscles, too to produce a total-body effect. To help get started with this routine, make sure that you use your hips in throwing the ball as opposed to your shoulders. Both your arms and legs should be able to throw the ball at the highest point possible your hands can reach to reduce exhaustion. When it comes to burpees, as much as possible, try not to stop, once you stop, you will have a hard time starting again.

Sit-ups and Lunges

3 rounds, 3 min., 2 min rest, AMRAP
15 sit-ups
15 lunges

This workout is an interval style WOD. It requires you to push as hard as you can for 3 mins., with 2 mins. of rest. This workout will help you develop cardio, this is used for endurance and training, so you can recover from fatigue in each interval, and although you won't recover fully in the 2 mins rest, you should at least come close to match your numbers in every round. If you feel very easy, modify it by adding some weight to the lunge or add 2 rounds to complete 5 rounds total.

The best thing about Cross Training is that you can modify every workout according to your strength. Beginners can alter weight, time and rep schemes for beginners. With this sport, you can work your way up. You will not lift 500 lbs right away. Cross Trainers come in all sizes and shapes, and improvements all depend on you. So don't get discouraged; rather, focus on becoming better each time you complete that next WOD.

Fran WOD

1 round for time

21	Thrusters
21	Pull-ups
15	Thrusters
15	Pull-ups
9	Thrusters

9 Pull-ups

According to experts, this is the most popular - yet dreaded - WOD. To perform this, begin in a standing position with a barbell against the shoulders. Then squat with the bar at shoulder level, with your palms facing up and extend your elbows out. While thrusting, return to standing with your weight over your head into a push press, use a fiery motion. Carry out 21 reps, then 21 pull-ups, then do the two exercises for fifteen reps, then 9, again without rest in between.

Breaking the 3 min margin is a big achievement. In the world finish, the top male scorer done 45 thrusters and 45 pull-ups in around 2 mins.

95 lbs for men is the standard weight for Fran and 65 lbs for women, but with Cross Training you need to know your limits and ease into the program. Many boxes help members finish the class where they learn the right form to complete the workouts safely before continuing with the WODs. And while other WODs recommend a specific weight, Cross Training does not require to be one size fits all.

You should learn to respect your limits and modify the weight for what you can handle safely.

Grace WOD

1 round For time:

30 Clean and Jerks

One of the most difficult movements in Cross Training is the Grace clean and jerks. They need strength, speed, flexibility, power and coordination.

The Cross Training athletes can finish Grace within 1 min. . The standard weight for women is 95 lbs and 135 lbs for men.

Annie WOD

50,40,30, 20, 10 reps (for time)

For	time:
50	Double-unders
50	Sit-ups
40	Double-unders
40	Sit-ups
30	Double-unders
30	Sit-ups
20	Double-unders
20	Sit-ups
10	Double-unders
10 Sit-ups	

One of the most difficult Cross Training workouts to learn is the double-under, and Annie makes you do 150 of them. There are some people who can easily pick it up, while some need many hours of practice to master it.

For beginners, use a jump rope that is chest height when standing on it, and begin jumping with two feet together. To perform a double-under jump a little bit higher and turn the jump rope times as fast as it goes under your feet twice before landing. As soon as you were able to work your way up to several double-unders in a row, you are now prepared for Annie.

Mary WOD

For 20 minutes:

5 Handstand push-ups

10 alternating One-legged squats,

15 Pull-ups

Mastering the handstand push-up is the first step for this WOD, which needs powerful shoulder strength. You can start by moving from the handstand position with your back on the wall, to handstand that faces the wall, and then progress to a handstand position without help from the wall, performing up to five reps. One-legged squats likewise called pistols is the next exercise. Hold onto the straps or rings, lean back before squatting down with one leg, while the other leg is straight out in front. Do this for 10 reps on every side before continuing with fifteen pull-ups. Then, squat without any help. Perform as many rounds as possible in twenty minutes, with a goal of 20 rounds.

Angie WOD

1 round for time
100 pull ups
100 push ups
100 sit ups
100 squats

Angie is a straightforward WOD that combines the basic bodyweight workouts for a full body killer workout. Complete all the reps before moving on to the next, shoot for twenty mins. Angie together with

Fran, is developed to be a benchmark WOD, which means you can use it to monitor how you progressed.

Cross Training WOD: Death by Clean and Jerks

1 clean jerk 1 min
2 clean and jerks 2 mins
3 clean and jerks 3 mins
4 clean and jerks 4 mins
135lbs men: 95lbs women

Cross Training WOD: Burpees and Running

10 burpees
100 meter run
9 burpess
100 meter run
8 burpees

Cross Training WOD: Jackie

1000 meter row
50 thrusters – 45 lbs men; 35 lbs women
30 pull-ups

Cross Training WOD: Row and Rest

Row and rest 4 rounds for time
500 meter row
3 mins rest

Cross Training WOD: Diane

21, 15, 9 reps for time
1 deadlift – 225 lbs for men: 155 lbs for women
2 handstand push ups

Cross Training WOD: Cross Training Games Open 12.4

150 wall balls – 20 lbs men to a 10 foot target
90 double unders
30 muscle ups

Chapter 9. Cross Training for Kids

Is Cross Training applicable for children? The answer is yes. Thousands and thousands of parents are enrolling their kids in Cross Training. Why? There are many reasons for this but the four topmost answers are these:

Physical benefits

Having a healthy body is achievable whatever the age may be. It is never too early to start being health conscious. The truth is, the earlier in life the person starts becoming concern about health, the better. Nobody is too young to benefit from Cross Training.

As mentioned, Cross Training is not just exercise. It is a wide variety of disciplines and it can serve as a foundation when these kids want to try other sports or activities later on. Cross Training includes weightlifting, calisthenics, and gymnastics, which are attractive to kids. Cross Training is equivalent to fun and fitness for kids.

Most parents are worried that they children might develop hulk-like muscles inappropriate for their age and body. In Cross Training for kids, strength training is being initiated. The focus is not to build up muscles but more of to strengthen them.

Studies have proven that strength training for children can be advantageous for them in terms of the following:

> ➢ Stronger muscles. The muscles would be able to endure more stress or difficulty. There is also increase in size. Kids will find everyday tasks to be easier like going to school, studying, helping in the house or garden, walking up the stairs, and other activities of daily living.

> ➢ Improved flexibility. The overall flexibility of the body is improved when the muscles are used to full range of motions. Kids who are not exposed to such activities cannot perform some of the basic skills that require flexibility. Being flexible prevents risk of back pains, strains and muscle pulls.

> ➢ Protection from injury. Cross Training kids have stronger muscles, ligaments and tendons that can withstand more stress.

They are les likely to be injured. Plus, Cross Training exercises can increase bone density, making the bones healthier and stronger.

➢ Prevents obesity. Obesity among young children and teenagers is rising at an alarming rate. Enrolling the kids at Cross Training can prevent unwanted weights from accumulating. There is decrease in waist measurement, too. It is noticeable that children who are enrolled in Cross Training classes are more careful in their selection of food. They tend to favor healthy meals.

➢ Defined muscle tone. Cross Training kids do not have flabby muscles. They look lean and fit.

➢ Posture – most kids tend to slouch and have poor posture. The exercises and activities of Cross Training will make them more conscious of their postures, at all times. Proper body mechanics are being taught and applied to keep them safe from injuries. The children get used to standing and sitting properly with their backs erect and with correct posture, at all times.

➢ Easy transition to other activities and sports. The variety of activities and exercises that Cross Training offers to its followers prepare them for whatever type of sports they may be interested in, later on.

Emotional benefits

Physical skills are not the only things that the children will learn in Cross Training. They will also work on sportsmanship, teamwork, leadership, self-discipline and manners. Cross Training can also impart to them how to follow directions, communicate with others and listen to people. These are things that are helpful in stabilizing the emotions of the children. These are skills that will aid the children to become successful in life, as they grow older.

Cross Training can help boost the self-confidence of these children. They begin to believe in themselves and in what they can do and achieve. They learn to rely on themselves. They are empowered.

Cross Training helps children to relate better with others. As they are exposed with other kids, they become more sociable and friendly.

Similar to the adult classes, the community among Cross Training kids is also close-knit.

The release of neurotransmitters such as serotonin, oxytocin and endorphins during Cross Training training would also prevent these children from becoming depressed and suicidal. These are the "feel-good" hormones that promote relaxation and feeling of happiness.

Healthy lifestyle

Children will be far from vices and unhealthy lifestyle when they engage in fitness early in life. They are more likely to adapt healthy living practices as they grow older. This can snowball and affect their lives in other areas such as school, family life, friends, and with other people. It will not come as a surprise if these kids end up as successful, well-rounded, responsible and happy adults.

Family relationship

Nowadays, it is a common occurrence for families to grow apart. Parents do not understand the generation of today and vice versa. Cross Training can bring the family together. When all the family members are into Cross Training, they share a common goal, that is, health of the whole family. They may not agree with other things but they can agree on how much fun Cross Training is. As they workout together, there is a special bond or connection that is being developed.

How to do Cross Training training for kids?

Classes are divided according to age groups. There is a class for 4-6 years old, 7-12 and for teenagers. Unlike the adult classes, the focus of learning centers on a circuit of pull-ups, pushups and squats.

> ➤ The main priority is safety, as children can hurt themselves and others while doing the exercises. This is primarily accomplished through close supervision of the coach. Children are also repeatedly instructed on how to be free from injury and stay safe. Next, the environment should also be safe for the children. It should be free from hazards.

Cross Training's Popularity Among Children

Why is Cross Training popular among children, even to those who are as young as 4 years old? It is simple – Cross Training is fun. For them, it is both business and pleasure. Who would not want to swing kettlebells, flip tires, do squats and dead lifts? These are equivalent to playing for kids, only it is more fun and healthier. The exercises are different for each day hence the children do not become bored with the routines.

The roles of the parents

Parents play major roles when it comes to the health of their children. Primarily, the child's nutrition is dependent on the parent's preference. Secondly, they also serve as models for their children to follow. Thus, when Mom and Dad are into exercise, it is not surprising that their offspring are interested in that, too. Thirdly, they can help the children do the exercises even at home. Lastly, parents are also the children's cheerleaders.

What is the best exercise for children?

Skill practice and games would work out well for children. There is running, jump roping, climbing and other body movements that can be used for the kids' exercises. When kids associate fun with fitness, exercise would be something that they would always look forward to.

As with the adults, the children can also learn the 10 general physical skills plus these skills are scalable, too. Cross Training aims to make everyone proficient in the following skills:

> - Cardiovascular/ respiratory endurance
> - Strength
> - Stamina
> - Speed
> - Agility
> - Flexibility
> - Balance
> - Accuracy
> - Coordination
> - Power

Here are some Cross Training workouts for the kids that they can enjoy even while they are at home.

> Bear Crawl. This is great for the shoulders, torso, arms and legs. Simply ask the kids to propel on their toes and arms without the knees touching the ground. Move right hand and left leg forward, followed by the left hand and right leg. Do this for several feet. Then do backward bear crawl and side to side. The kids will totally love this fun exercise. You can add more fun to activity by allowing them to growl like bears or making them wear their bear hats.

> Crab Walk. This exercise improves coordination of large muscles and promotes whole body strength. This is like the opposite of the bear crawl. The kids are on their all fours too but their face and body face the sky. Ask the children to lift the body high from the ground. Arch the back as far back as they can. Their glutes or bottoms should be tight. Do not allow the butts to slum down while they are doing the crabwalk. Let the children go forward and backward. They can do 8-12 repetitions of this exercise.

> Side to side hops for one minute. Ask the kids to form a line. Then, instruct them to hop using one leg until they reach the finish line. Going back to the starting line, they should use the other leg to hop. This should be accomplished in one minute.

> Underhand ball toss. Using a basketball, toss the ball to the child and he should be able to catch it. Afterwards, he should do the same to you. Do this exercise in one minute. Count how many times this exercise is done in a minute. This can be used as baseline information to monitor the progress of the child.

> Jump rope. Let the child jump rope for one minute. Count the number of jumps he made. Kids of all ages love this game. One can make this more exciting when another child would join in the one doing the exercise. They should be able to jump rope together.

> Monkey bar hang. Allow the kid to hang for 30 seconds in a monkey bar. This activity helps strengthen the back, core and grip of the child. At the beginning, one can support the child by holding him up to the bar just to decrease the pressure from his arms. When he is strong enough to do the exercise on his own, then it is time to add more seconds to the exercise.

Cross Training is incorporated into the life of the child in the form of fun and play and games. Cross Training can bring out the best in children.

Chapter 10. More Challenging WODs Cross Training For Your Abs, Thighs, Butt and Arms

Maybe you are looking for a more challenging WOD Cross Training, here are some that will help you build muscles on your abs, thigh, butt and arms. Just like the WODs for beginners, these workouts will test your endurance, speed and strength, and you will be completing these exercises in a group setting. These workouts vary from extremely difficult though.

Filthy 50

Challenge time: 25 mins.
50 reps
50 box jumps
50 jumping pullups
50 kettlebell swings
50 walking lunge steps
50 knees to elbows
50 reps of push press
50 back extensions
50 wallballs
50 burpees
50 double unders

Filthy 50 is a vicious series of demanding exercises that is likely to appear endless to you if you have never done this before. These reps are done as quickly as you can. The box jumps are completed using a 24-inch box. Push press is performed using 45 pounds. Wallballs is carried out with the use a 20 pound ball. Challenge time 25 minutes.

Murph

Run one mile
100 pullups
200 pushups
300 squats
Run another mile

This is quite simple but pushes your body to the limit with its persistence. Carry out the exercises as fast as you can. If you want, you can modify the pullups. Cross Trainingers carry out this exercise with a weighted vest. This workout is named after Navy Lt. Michael Murphy.

Challenge   Time:
Go for 40 minutes or less, but up to 45 minutes is still strong. - -

The Seven

7 rounds
7 handstand pushups
7 thrusters
7 knee to elbows
7 deadlifts
7 burpees
7 kettlebell swings
7 pullups

This workout is carried out as fast as possible in a cycle for 7 rounds. A 135 pound is used in thrusters. Deadlifts uses a 245 pound lift.

The Ryan

5 rounds
7 muscle ups
21 burpees

This workout is done as fast as possible. It is named after the Firefighter Ryan Hummert, who died while on duty. Complete the workout less than 25 minutes. Expert Cross Trainers can complete this below 15 minutes.

King Kong

3 rounds
1 deadlift

2 muscle ups
3 squat cleans
4 handstand pushups

Complete three rounds as fast as possible. The deadlift at 455 pounds and the squat cleans at 250 pounds. The challenge time is 5 minutes.

Cross Training Circuit Workout

Dumbbell Swing

This workout targets the abs, hamstrings, shoulders, butt and back. Stand with feet a little bit wider than the shoulder-width apart, hold a single dumbbell with hands in front of thighs.

Bend the knees slightly as you hinge forward from the hips until back is almost parallel to the floor and then swing the dumbbell behind you between legs.
Then drive through heels as fast as you can and push hips forward to straighten the legs, swinging the dumbbell overhead in an upward arc, arm straight. Repeat right away. Do 20 reps.

Elevator

- This workout targets the legs, shoulders, butt and hips.
- Stand as you face the chair, a dumbbell in each hand.
- Position the right foot on the seat and carry dumbbells by the shoulders, with palms facing each other.
- Stand up on seat on right leg, lifting the bent left knee as you press dumbbells overhead.
- Lower the left foot to floor, then lunge back with your right leg. Jump up, switching legs in the midair to land in lunge with your right leg forward. Do it again, positioning the left foot on the seat. Do ten reps, alternating sides.
- To make it simpler, leave arms by sides while performing the workout.

Turkish Get-Up

- This WOD targets the abs, butt, hamstrings, triceps and obliques.
- Hold a dumbbells in the right hand, lie on the floor face up, with the right knee bent and foot flat on the ground, and left leg extended, raise your right arm on the ceiling and extend your left arm out to your side with the palms touching the floor.
- Keep the right arm pointing up throughout, then press on the left forearm to lift your torso off the floor and then press into left palm and the right heel to lift the hips.
- Bring the left leg behind the body, kneel on the left knee and then stand up. Then reverse the motion back to start.
- Do three reps, before switching sides. Repeat.

Power Deck Squat

- This workout targets legs, abs and butt
- Stand with feet shoulder – width apart, hold ends of a single dumbbell with both hands in front of the chest, bend elbows by the sides.
- Keep the dumbbell close to the chest throughout, lower into a deep squat. Then sit on the floor and maintain a tuck position with the chin toward chest, roll on the middle of the back and then upper back.
- Roll forward with momentum to return to squat, and then jump.
- Perform six reps.
- Make it simpler. Rather than jumping up, return to standing
- Make it harder. Press the dumbbell overhead before you jump from the squat position.

Inchworm to Grasshopper

- Targets the back, chest, arms, abs and shoulders
- Stand with feet apart, then hinge forwards at hips, with your back flat, and position palms on the floor.
- Walk hands forward in a full plank position
- Put left leg diagonally underneath the body toward the right hip. Return to plank, switch legs, do it again.

- Alternate sides again, then walk hands back to meet feet to start again. Do ten reps.
- Make it simpler. Bend knees a little bit on the walk-out.

Handstand Push-Up

- It focuses on the triceps, abs and shoulders.
- Kneel on all fours on the floor with your back to a chair. Position balls on feet atop seat and then keep arms extended, straighten the legs so that hips rise in an inverted-V pike spot.
- Bend the elbows slowly to lower head near the floor
- Push the palms to extend arms fully
- Perform five reps.
- Make it simpler. Rest knees and shins on the chair or do the move with feet on the floor.
- Make it simpler. Bend knees a little bit on the walk-out.

Kalsu

5 burpees
135 pounds thrusters on the minute

- Your goal is to complete 100 total thrusters. At the start of every minute perform 5 burpees, for the rest of the minute. Carry out as many thrusters as you can during that time.

- At the start of the next minute do 5 burpees and then maximum rep thrusters and so on until you complete one hundred total thrusters.

Chapter 11. Incorporating Cross Training To Your Workout Regimen And Lifestyle

The best way to experience Cross Training is by joining a Cross Training gym. This is especially beneficial if you are a beginner. The instructors will be able to teach you the fundamental moves and correct your form.

How to find a Cross Training gym

If you live in the city, there are probably a lot of Cross Training gyms in your area, but remember that some gyms are better than others. There are many factors to consider when choosing a gym. You need to find a gym that employs qualified and trained coaches. You should be able to see and check their certifications. Cross Training level 1 certification means that the coach has trained long and know how to teach the basic movements and how to scale them. However, he/she will not teach you how to deal with injuries or any advance movements.

Cross Training level 2 is the next level and it involves advance training and coaching. There are also specialty seminars that include specific classes such as gymnastics, lifting or running.

Aside from the coaches, you should also look into their programming. Cross Training programs can be very random which means that they may plan workouts that target the same muscle groups and not give your muscles enough time to recover. Make sure to check their website to know their WOD. If they do heavy shoulder movements for three days in a row, then they do not know how to program well.

You should also consider the environment in the gym. The coaches and other members should also be nice and welcoming. A good Cross Training community is essential for your success.

How to do Cross Training at home

If you find a good Cross Training gym but cannot attend most of their workouts, you can still follow their workouts by looking into their website. Working out at home might feel different from working out in a gym, but it is better than not working out at all.

Working out at home is also a great alternative if you want to save money, and if you already have the right equipment. You can also modify the workouts to fit your current fitness level.

Doing Cross Training at home is possible but you have to be smart about it since there will be no one to check your form.

Incorporating Cross Training to Mass Training

Incorporating different variety into your workout is essential to keep your body in the best shape. Cross training also optimize your benefits. Integrating Cross Training into your mass training is one of the best ways to increase muscle size.

Mass training builds muscles using free weights, and is usually done by bodybuilders and weight lifters. Both athletes can benefits from doing Cross Training. Many WOD includes power lifts and kettle bell exercise that can improve mass training.

You can combine the two by interchanging your workout routine by following Cross Training WOD and cycle the moves into your regular training. This can help you build muscles mass to keep you lean and healthy. If you are new to lifting, it might be necessary to consult an instructor to ensure that you have proper form and do not accidentally hurt yourself. Remember to gradually increase the weights that you use as you become accustomed to the training program.

Incorporating Cross Training to Triathlon training

Cross Training is great to incorporate into strength and endurance training. Triathletes can incorporate Cross Training into their routine to improve their performance. It allows the athlete to maximize workout time by increasing endurance stamina and power.

You can incorporate Cross Training by following a specific training schedule which includes three days of workout followed by one day or rest. Aim for 4-5 workouts in a week. Make sure that you perform functional movements and constantly try different moves to maximize results.

Train each of the discipline of triathlon twice in a week. For example, you can run on Monday and Thursday, swim on Tuesday and Friday and cycle on Wednesday and Saturday.

You can modify your Cross Training workout according to your regular workout. Make sure that you interchange between cardio and strength training to avoid overworking the same muscle groups.

It is also beneficial to keep your workout session 45 minutes to one hour long. The short amount of time lets you increase the intensity and reduce the risk of injury. Lastly, track your performance to see how much progress you are making. You can record time, heart rate as well as problems encountered during the run. Do not forget to give your body enough rest. Triathlon training is tedious and can push your endurance to the limit. Make sure to rest to ensure that your muscles recover. You should also never forget to eat whole foods and minimize processed food to get the most nutrients out of your food.

Incorporating Cross Training to running

Runners might think that their legs are strong but they are only accustomed to one pattern of movement. Running involves a repetitive movement that only involves the legs. Cross Training on the other hand involves your whole body and can strengthen you from head to toe. Cross Training training that involves power lifting and gymnastics can help in sprinting and muscle twitching. Cross Training can also prevent workout plateaus that are common when you only focus on one form of exercise. You can incorporate Cross Training in between your running schedule. Make sure that you join a gym that assists you through every move. Good Cross Training programs enable you to strengthen your muscles and improve your overall performance. How often you do Cross Training depends on your goals. If running is your main focus, you can supplement it with 2-3 Cross Training classes in a week.

Incorporating Cross Training to martial arts

Cross Training can help you improve your martial arts abilities. Cross Training can help you achieve overall fitness. The intervals of heavy lifting, gymnastics and speed work can make you fitter and stronger for your martial arts training. Martial arts athletes need to develop endurance so that they can continue fighting.

Cross Training can also help athletes improve their explosive power. People who regularly incorporate Cross Training into their routine develop incredible power. It gives you the ability to release strength with speed and accuracy.

Martial arts athletes need to be in their best shape and peak condition. Cross Training can help by consciously challenging the body to become stronger. It also improves mental strength and discipline that is needed in martial arts. It can help you maintain focus even after having serious physical injuries.

You can incorporate Cross Training into your routine by doing it 2-3 times in a week in between your regular martial arts training.

How to create your own Cross Training workout

Cross Training workouts can be described as high intensity and short in duration. You can start to develop your own Cross Training workout after understanding the main program.

Remember the basic three:

The basic three modalities of Cross Training include gymnastics, weightlifting and metabolic conditioning. Gymnastic moves include air squats, pushups and pull ups. Metabolic conditioning is exercises that improve your cardiovascular health. Example of exercises includes rowing and jumping. Strength training involves equipments like dumbbells and kettle bells.

Cross Training usually follows a three-day training followed by one day of rest. The first day should only include one modality, the second day includes two modalities and all modalities should be incorporated during the third day.

Make it simple

You can make your workouts simple by focusing on one modality and choosing a single exercise. For example, if you focus on metabolic conditioning, you can go for a run or cycle. If you are focusing on weight lifting exercise, you can repeat the same exercise using different sets of weights.

Double it

As you become more comfortable in your workouts, you can start incorporating complex movements or matching two exercises from different modalities. For instance, you can pair squats with pull-ups to target more muscle groups at once. Remember that you should always monitor your intensity and minimize the amount of rest in between.

Triple it

You can also select three exercises from different modalities and complete as many rounds as you can in 15 minutes. This helps workout your entire body and keeps the workout exciting. The intensity of your workouts should be between moderate to high.

Chapter 12. Cross Training Games

Cross Training games started way back 2007. It was sponsored by Cross Training Inc with the goal of determining who is the "fittest on earth". According to the proponents of Cross Training games, there is really no sport or contest that measures the true test of fitness, hence the creation of this activity, which is now being hailed as America's fastest growing sports.

In 2011, an online format of the competition was started. In here, competitors from all over the world submit their entries with scores online. From there, the winner will proceed to the Cross Training game, which has been held at California for several years now.

The game is categorized into individual man, woman and team. Contestants should at least be 14 years old. It has three stages. These are:

1. Cross Training Games Open. The open is set for five weeks with five workout competitions. It is held among Cross Training affiliates all over the world during the early spring. The workouts are being released online every Thursday. The athletes or contestants have up to the following Monday to pass or submit their scores online.

2. Cross Training Games Regionals. This second stage is held for three weekends in May. Those athletes who did very well during the Open stage combine and compete to qualify for the last stage, which is the Cross Training Games.

3. Cross Training Games. From thousands of athletes, the list is narrowed down to 40 men and 40 women that will compete for the title of "Fittest on Earth".

The mechanics of the game include competitors not being aware of the activities prior to the contest. Therefore, they are advised to be ready for anything. The games include the standard aerobic, gymnastic movements and weightlifting. Surprised activities commonly not part of Cross Training exercises are also incorporated, such as ocean swim, softball throw or triathlon. Why is it done this way? In order to test the "fitness" of an individual, he must be able to survive something that he has not trained for. A person is considered truly fit when he has the ability to perform unknown and challenging tasks.

The Games are changed every year. This way, there would be no way for the contestants to prepare for the event itself. What they would be doing is to prepare themselves by making their body fit and healthy. That way, whatever the challenge may be, they would be able to perform it.

How to prepare for the competition?

1. One should start with self-assessment. What are the skills that one has? What are his weaknesses and strengths? Is he mentally ready for the competition? The contestant should determine his own strengths and weaknesses. Afterwards, he should train to improve his weaknesses while maintaining his strengths.

2. Have more time for training. Training does not only happen during classes. If the contestant is determined to win in the competition, he must find and make time to train even outside his classes' schedule.

3. Train with athletes who are better. Contestants should aim to improve his skill and he can accomplish that when there is another athlete who is better than him. He would learn a lot from others who are performing more advanced workouts than him.

4. Be under a qualified and good coach. The coach could help choose or make the program that would enhance one's strengths and improve one's weaknesses. He could also guide the contestant on the right execution of the workouts.

5. Be prepared mentally. A contestant who has given time to do mental training has the edge over those who did not. He could visualize the actions that he would take. He could encourage himself especially during difficult workouts. He could be positive even when everything is going wrong.

6. Do not forget to enjoy. The competition is not designed to stress one out. It is designed to test how fit one is. If the athlete takes it so seriously that he does not enjoy the trainings and practices

71

anymore, then he totally misses the whole point of the competition. The real prize is not the title or the money. It is the health of the individual.

The competition itself may be stressful but it does not have to affect one negatively. All that is needed is to be ready physically, emotionally and intellectually.

How to join the Open?

1. Register – one can do this online. If this is the first time, the applicant should create an account on Cross Training's webpage. Former applicants just need to login using their old email and password. The applicant will be asked to fill up a form.

2. Pay the registration fee. There is a fee of $20 for athletes residing in America, Canada, Europe and Australia. Athletes from other parts of the world must pay the $10 registration fee.

3. One could also join in his affiliate or affiliate's team. A different form would need to be filled up.

Submission of entry

During the Open competition, a workout will be given and the athlete needs to perform the task and submit his entry via online. There are two ways one can have his performance validated – score submission and video.

In score submission, one has to perform the workout before an affiliate. It will be the applicant's discretion to select the affiliate. He has to submit the name of the judge, his score and if applicable, the tiebreak time.

If the contestant chooses video, he has to record his performance of the given workout and upload the link to the video. As with score submission, the contestant will have to encode his score and tiebreak time, if applicable.

Take note that late submissions would not be accepted under any circumstances. In case one is experiencing technical difficulties, he could send an email informing the organizer of the situation. As long as the email is before the deadline of submission, it would be entertained. However, late reports will not be considered.

Also, it is the responsibility of the contestant to ensure that all data needed are encoded in the entry, for example, the scores, name of affiliates, and others. Entries with incomplete information will also not be considered.

Validation of the entry

A validation deadline is given and only the Affiliate Manager where one has performed or completed the workout can validate the score of the contestant. How? The Affiliate Manager has to login into his account and do the validation of the contestant's score. The contestant will know if the Affiliate Manager has done his part, as the score should appear on the leaderboard once validation has been completed.

Lessons of the Games

For most spectators, Cross Training Games is another way to say how good or how skilled a person is. However, for the athletes or contestants themselves, this is more than just a competition. It is life lessons.

Lesson #1 You can be better

The competition's main goal is to acknowledge the fittest person on the Earth. Who is this fittest person? He is not the one who is strongest physically. After all, the challenges being given do not use the body alone. The athlete must also be mentally prepared plus he must be able to think of strategies of executing the tasks. This is a competition that would bring out the very best of the person.

It is during practices and training that this life lesson is usually learned. As the athlete goes through the process of becoming fit, he realizes that he can always push his body to improve. Even if he has perfected a certain workout, he could still do something better. Why? It is because man by nature always aims to outdo himself. There is always room for improvement.

If the athlete will not do his part, other competitors would surely beat him. Experiencing defeat because others are better is not the real defeat. It is about not giving his best to the endeavor. He knows he could have done better. An athlete may be bested by others but as long as he knows within his heart that he has done his best, then he knows that he is a winner also.

Lesson #2 Do not forget the most important thing – have fun.

Cross Training in itself symbolizes fun in fitness. However, many athletes, in the process of wanting to win in the games, forget the fun part. This is a big error. When the fun part is removed, Cross Training (and health for that matter) becomes burdensome. One can be physically fit and lean but not happy. This is not true health.

Cross Training Games is a serious business but it does not necessarily mean that one should be so serious that there is no enjoyment anymore. That is very similar to wanting very much to be successful in life only to miss out on real success. For example, people would work very hard to accumulate wealth. At the end of their life, they discover that wealth is not the real treasure.

Do not make this same mistake with Cross Training Games. It is not the medal or even the title of being the fittest that is the target here. It is about the person achieving total health and having fun doing it.

With this attitude, practice and training become easier for the athlete. Why? The athlete is relaxed. The motivation is right. Winning is important but it is not everything. In fact, just to be in the Cross Training class makes one a winner already. All contestants are winners in their own rights.

Lesson #3 – Learning to see the big picture

The competition is viewed by many as a very important event in the life of a Cross Trainingter. It is actually a much-awaited event for them. However, do not be deceived. The competition is not the big picture. What is? It is actually the daily practices and trainings. It is the little things in life that make up the big picture.

Winning is not for a day only. Therefore, giving one's best is not exclusive during the competition day only. It is supposed to be practiced everyday. Cross Training encourages its followers to always give their best, not for them to gain a title or an award. It is for them to realize that excellence is a lifestyle.

Final thoughts on Cross Training Games

The game is about the athlete himself. It is not about beating other athletes to the title. It is not about proving to the world that he is the strongest or the smartest. It is about health and how one can be healthy and have fun at the same time.

Cross Training Games is also about other athletes. They are not against you. They are not your enemies. They are in fact part of one's family. Hence, one rejoices when a new record is achieved or even when the other athlete wins. Why? It's a healthy competition. It is just like being happy when your brother gets promoted in his job. His victory is the family's victory, too. That's the same way with Cross Training Games.

Chapter 13. Cross Training FAQs

The mere mention of Cross Training can conjure images of sweaty bodies, heavy weights and incredible physique. More and more people are interested to join a Cross Training gym. It attracts athletes, fitness enthusiasts and cross trainers. Here are some of the frequently asked questions about Cross Training.

What is the difference between a Cross Training box and a gym?

Commercial gyms are usually packed with rows of exercise machines and weight racks. In a box, there is a smaller array of barbells to make way for a wider space for lifting platform. You may also see equipments such as medicine balls, kettle bells and even climbing ropes. In a Cross Training box, a great community is also developed. People who train at the same time end up being friends who support each other.

Who is Cross Training for?

Cross Training tends to appeal more to a certain group of people. These include people who are new to weight training, fitness buffs and athletes. Cross Training is also great for people who likes to experience community support and enjoys a competitive atmosphere.

Can Cross Training help me achieve my goals?

Cross Training is great to add to your regular workout routine. It can help you become stronger, fitter and faster. However, you have to remember that Cross Training does not focus on a single athletic ability alone.

Are the workouts too difficult?

One of the best things about Cross Training is that you can adjust it depending on your physical ability. If you cannot complete the workouts as prescribed, then do what you can. For example, if you cannot do pull ups, you can do ring rows instead. If you cannot jump in a 36 inch box then start with 20 inches.

Remember that no one should force yourself to do something that your body is not prepared for. Make sure that you train constantly to improve your abilities. Cross Training is also a great way to pin point your weakness.

What should I expect during the first few weeks?

The first thing that you have to expect before joining is that the workouts will challenge your body. You'll encounter new varieties of exercises and exert more energy that you are used to. Do not be afraid of learning the mechanics and trying new things since you will improve faster than you expect.

How to choose a coach?

There are a lot of qualified Cross Training instructors but you also have to look for one that you feel comfortable working together with. After making sure that they have the right certification, you should also ask about their background and training. It is important that your trust your trainer completely.

Is it dangerous?

Just like any sport, Cross Training also come with its own dangers but it is usually not as dangerous as you might think.

In a workout, you might be told to complete exercises as fast as you can or complete as many repetitions in the given amount of time. It is really easy to lose proper form just so you can finish the workout faster. Improper form makes you more susceptible to injuries.

Cross Training also appeals to certain kinds of individuals, namely those who constantly want to push their body beyond the limit. The nature of Cross Training also nurtures competition and may lead people to do more than they are able. This is a great thing if you want to improve but there is also a risk of overdoing it.

You should also be aware of a medical condition known as rhabdomyolysis. It happens where a person pushes their body too much and too fast, that the muscles fibers in their body break down and seeps into the bloodstream, which can poison the kidneys. This is the reason proper rest is very important in Cross Training. Be smart and keep your safety in mind.

Is it worth than the investment?

Joining a Cross Training gym is more expensive than commercial gyms because the classes include few people. It is quite similar to other group classes like yoga or Pilates. Also, a single workout can target all of your muscle groups in just a short amount of time. Get the most of your money by signing up for membership and showing up at the gym regularly.

Do I have to eat Paleo?

There are no specific rules that say that you need to eat Paleo although many Cross Training athletes swear by the diet. Remember that what you eat can definitely affect your performance. Paleo is healthier than the standard diet rich in carbohydrates and processed food. It encourages the consumption of whole foods and eliminates wheat, grains, sugar and processed goods.

What is it with the shoes and long socks?

Just like other sports, Cross Training also have their own specializes equipment. Long socks are helpful if you do multiple rope ascends, box jumps and dead lifts. Good shoes are also essential but do not need to choose a specific brand or style for Cross Training.

Can Cross Training make me lose weight?

The energy used in a single Cross Training workout can burn a lot of calories but you also have to be mindful of your diet. If you eat right and combine it with Cross Training, then you will be able to notice a great difference within just 30 days.

Chapter 14. Common Myths and Misconceptions Concerning Cross Training

This chapter of the book addresses some of the myths and misconceptions about Cross Training.

A. Cross Training workouts are insane and too difficult. Also, they are not intended for those who are too old/too young.

This is definitely not true. Some might find the Cross Training.com website a little bit intimidating because of the pictures and workouts, one of the most amazing things about Cross Training is all of the workouts are infinitely scalable. You might be wondering, what does this mean? It implies that you only do what you can do. Cross Training will never put you in a position in which you are at risk of hurting yourself. For example, in a particular WOD, the prescribed weight is 95# for women and 135# for men. There are cases where no one will perform the prescribed weight. Most people will scale down to a safer and more manageable weight. Cross Training trains everyone from kids to senior citizens because they make the WOD suit you and vice versa. In short, it is safe for all ages. With Cross Training, you are expected to perform the exercise as hard as you safely can so you can be at your best but not at the expense of your health.

B. Cross Training is too expensive.

If you check out other gyms, and compare Cross Training monthly rates you might think that it is too expensive. But look deeper on what others are offering and what Cross Training offers. At Cross Training you are getting a licensed trainer to help you complete your workout safely every time you walk in the door. The personal trainer has been licensed to teach you how to lift weights properly and safely and also get the most out of you to be at your very best. Normally, personal trainers will charge you by the hour. If you check out other gyms, this is not included to your membership fees, so that cheap $19 that other gyms offer will turn into a $150 + monthly charge. These gyms are making money off of their trainers and the protein shakes and other stuff they sell while you are in their gym. At Cross Training you can get a personal trainer included in your monthly fee and they will not force you to buy supplements. They believe that you can get everything you need with the right diet and they will teach how.

C. You need to get fit first before joining Cross Training

You join a fitness program to get in shape and lose weight. Cross Training knows what it takes to achieve your goals, this is the reason why they exist. They will help you lose weight and gain muscle safely. That is their job and that is the reason why you join in the first place. Because Cross Training exercises are scalable, it does not matter what fitness level you are when you join. They start you off based on your fitness level and build up from there.

D. Working out will get you bulky and too big

There are two things that you need to do in order you to get big, particularly women. One is to pick up very heavy weight on a regular basis. This is not something that people do very often. Definitely, Cross Training is concerned about your strength and they do lift heavy sometimes. But this is not their main concern. Two is to have a high calorie diet. For many in order to gain good muscle mass it takes a lot of effort in eating the appropriate foods. This is also not the main concern of Cross Training. The majority of the exercises provides your muscles with more contractile potential and not muscle mass.

E. Don't have the time to do the exercises

Most Americans are wasting more than two to four hours a day watching TV and around 30 minutes waiting on someone. If you spent two hours in watching movie while riding a bike or played or walked on an elliptical, then yes, you do not have the time to work for that type of exercise. The majority of the workouts may take up to 2 hours by performing thirty to sixty minutes of weight training and spending more time on a treadmill, elliptical or bike machine. With Cross Training, you only need an hour or less to complete your workout.

F. It is best to do workouts on your own at home with a video

The success rate with these types of workout is a gloomy 15%. If there is no one holding you accountable, there is a tendency that you let stuff that is not comfortable, such as workout, fall to the wayside. Credit to those who can continue with it on the right track, but still fall way short of what dependable, structured program can provide. People need extra pressure in order to stick with the program, regardless whether it is a workout partner, or a scheduled session time where you need to attend, an appointment to keep, or a group of individuals to workout with. It is referred to as accountability. That's what will make it work.

G. Only former athletes can handle this

The first time you walk into the Olympic Village, you might get intimidated by so many shirtless, well-sculpted men, and well-shaped women everywhere. But they are not at all athletes. They might have played sports during their high school days, but this is not high school, so take it easy. Anyone can perform this workout and you will not be chosen last.

Cross Training is for everybody. There are some people who join the classes and have never done exercises before. There are also some who are 80 lbs overweight, but manage to lose 50 lbs in the first 7 months just by joining Cross Training classes. There are also some people who attain serious back injuries who are not carrying out movements that they were not able to do before due to their injury.

Conclusion

Thank you again for purchasing this book!

I hope this book was able to help you to understand Cross Training better.

The next step is to try these WODs.

Finally, if you enjoyed this book, please take the time to share your thoughts and post a review on Amazon. We do our best to reach out to readers and provide the best value we can. Your positive review will help us achieve that. It'd be greatly appreciated!

Thank you and good luck!

Made in the USA
San Bernardino, CA
14 July 2015